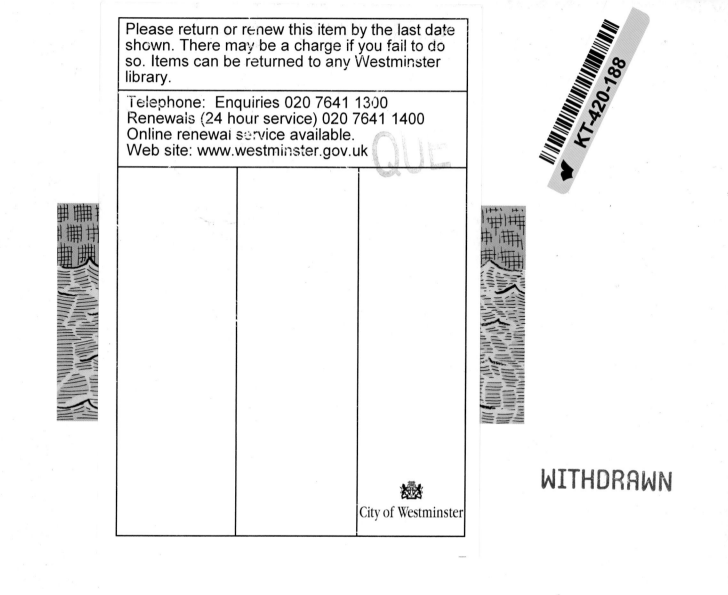

For Marissa, Eva and Jonathan, now that you're older M.B.

For Alison, thank you for the great design work and much needed advice over the years N.M.

First published in 2012 by Hodder Children's Books
This paperback edition first published in 2013

Hodder Children's Books, 338 Euston Road, London, NW1 3BH
Hodder Children's Books Australia, Level 17/207 Kent Street, Sydney, NSW 2000

A catalogue record of this book is available from the British Library.

ISBN: 978 1 444 90248 8
10 9 8 7 6 5 4 3 2 1

Printed in China

Hodder Children's Books is a division of Hachette Children's Books, an Hachette UK Company
www.hachette.co.uk

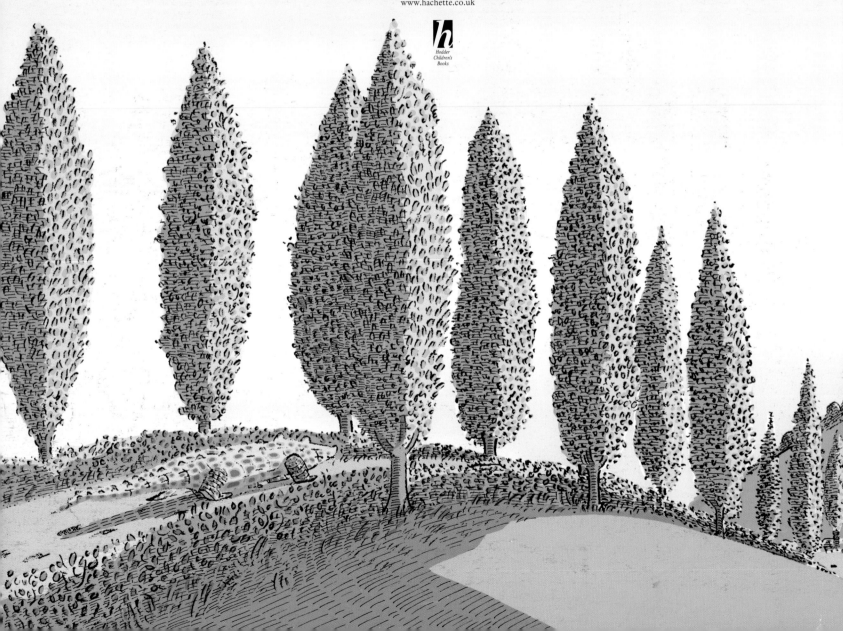

WHEN THE
ALLIGATOR
CAME TO PLAY

Written by **Mara Bergman** ✱ Illustrated by **Nick Maland**

When the alligator
came *creeping*,
creeping,
creeping down the street,

were the people scared?

YOU BET THEY WERE!

Windows were closed
and doors were locked.

Parents and children alike
were SHOCKED.
And no one knew quite
what to do...

In a corner of town
    where children have fun
boys and girls shouted,
    'Watch out!' and 'LET'S RUN!'

as one great-big alligator
        came into view,
    nudged the gate open
        and trotted straight through.

Snip, snap! Snip, snap! Snip, snap!

What ever should the children do?

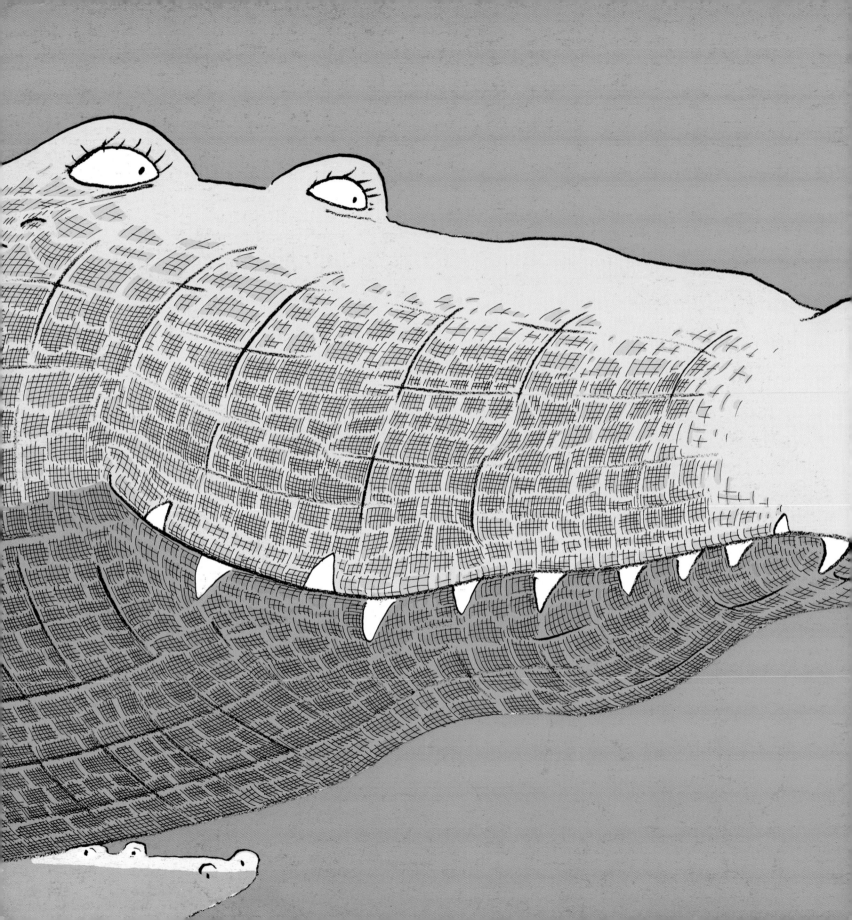

Marissa yelled, 'Why are you here?'
Eva cried, 'Don't get too near!'
And Jonathan didn't know
quite what to say,
so he kept extremely quiet.

Then they saw someone wriggly
and what a surprise
to see lots of sharp teeth
and such bright shiny eyes!

'Isn't it sweet?' Marissa asked.
'It wants to play!' said Eva at last.

Jonathan didn't know quite what to say,
so he kept extremely quiet.

The alligators **glanced, pranced, danced** all around, overjoyed to discover this exciting playground!

Girls and boys were now running away –
   but one little alligator wanted to play!
So Marissa and Eva and Jonathan
   showed it the way.

Together they slid down

and flew up

high into the air.

They climbed and
they clambered,
first here

and then there,
helping and holding the baby with care.

The boys and girls watched
afraid that they might
see the alligator

start to bite!

(But it didn't!)

So now what did the children do?

Why, they said to the others,
'Come and play too!'

So everybody **rolled**
and **wiggled,**
bounced
and **giggled,**

and then did some **swirling**
and **whirling**
and **twirling** until

Jonathan shouted out,
'STOP!'
because...

...another alligator
appeared at the gate.
Was it looking for DINNER?
Did it just want to play?

Not exactly – but the children
jumped out of its way!

Then the alligator baby
ran to its father
and everyone watched
as they hugged each other.

By now the day was turning to night,
the time when all alligators slip out of sight.

'That was great!' said Marissa.

Eva gave a great sigh.

Jonathan tried very hard not to cry

as they waved and watched and called,

'**Goodbye!**'

and the alligators went strutting, strutting,

strutting down the street...

...all the way back home.